FINDING YOUR FIRST HORSE

How to Buy a Horse Without Losing Your Mind (Or Money)

MEREDITH HILL

© 2022 Finding Your First Horse : How to Buy a Horse without Losing Your Mind (or Money)

All rights reserved. No part of the book may be reproduced in any shape or form without permission from the publisher.

This guide is written from a combination of experience and high-level research. Even though we have done our best to ensure this book is accurate and up to date, there are no guarantees to the accuracy or completeness of the contents herein.

ISBN: 9781953714503

DOWNLOAD YOUR FREE CHECKLIST NOW!

Horse owners are often accused of having too much stuff, and yet we always find ourselves without that One Thing that we really, really need. This list is intended to keep the new horse owner organized so you have a head start on your own collection of "stuff."

Go to https://free.meredithhillbook.com/checklist to download it for free

REVIEWS

Reviews and feedback help improve this book and the author. If you enjoy this book, we would greatly appreciate it if you could take a few moments to share your opinion and post a review on Amazon.

Download The Audio Version of This Book for Free! If you love listening to audiobooks on-the-go or enjoy the narration as you read along I have great news for you. You can download this book for **FREE** just by signing up for a FREE 30-day audible trial. Just use the links below

FOR AUDIBLE UK:

https://tinyurl.com/4ze6thhu

FOR AUDIBLE US:

https://tinyurl.com/2ma8erme

ALSO BY MEREDITH HILL

Before Your Horse Comes Home

http://mybook.to/horses

CONTENTS

INTRODUCTION	7
CHAPTER 1 : WHAT KIND OF HORSE DO YOU WANT?	9
Building Your Dream Horse	10
The Dream Horse's Dream Job	11
CHAPTER 2 : WHAT KIND OF HORSE DO YOU NEED?	12
Size	13
Temperament	15
Skills and Training	16
CHAPTER 3 : WHAT KIND OF HORSE CAN YOU AFFORD?	20
Author's Anecdote: What If It Doesn't Work Out?	23
CONCLUSION	25

INTRODUCTION

A horse is a strange thing, and I mean that in every sense of the world. If you've read my current books on the topic– *Before Your Horse Comes Home: Introductory Horse Care for Beginners* and *I Have a Horse… Now What : How Grooming, Training, Riding, and Equine Competitive Activities Can Build a Lifelong Bond*- you've met the acquaintance of my wacky equine companions, Red and Belle. You've also learned about my own experience with horses which spans nearly four decades and several states. I have what seems like an endless trail of weird horse stories… mainly because horses are all very different.

Perhaps I repeat it too often, but each horse truly is an individual with a personality, likes and dislikes, and loads of opinions. This isn't to necessarily anthropomorphize horses as humans trapped in equine bodies, but to state that all sentient creatures do have their own ideas about how things should be. They like this food, but not this one. They have itchy places, "don't touch" spots, favorite locations to take a sun or mud bath, and so on.

In *Before Your Horse Comes Home: Introductory Horse Care for Beginners*, we look at what a horse needs to be happy and healthy under your care. Whether that was your own backyard barn or selecting a boarding stable, we walked through the steps of general care and cleanliness. In *I Have a Horse… Now What : How Grooming, Training, Riding, and Equine Competitive Activities Can Build a Lifelong Bond*, we examine the process of doing things with your horse, from learning to communicate with your horse to studying various disciplines and competing with your equine companion.

But, what's the process that takes us from being a mere "equine enthusiast" to a full-blown "horse owner?" In some cases, it happens almost accidentally with a handshake or a hug. On the other hand, it can take people years to meet their ideal horse buddy.

People who haven't spent a lot of time with horses often figure "a horse is a horse (of course, of course)." Big, four legs, lots of hair, huge teeth, right? True... to a point. Most people who are looking to add a horse to their lives are looking for a reason. For example, they may want to compete at a certain level of an equine sport or ride around at home and on trails without feeling anxious or afraid. Perhaps they want a small pony to pull a little cart around just for fun. Or, maybe they want a personable lawn ornament.

Some people are interested in buying a horse out of a lingering desire to have a horse in their immediate vicinity, despite having no background in horses. If this describes you, I can certainly understand, as I've been "horse crazy" since I was able to comprehend what a horse was. But if you fall in this category, I urge you to read this, my other books, and as many resources you can find to guide you in the process. I have included quite a few resources in each of my full sized books to get you started. Horses aren't easy– they're fragile both inside and out, and each one is very different. However, we all start from the beginning, and educating yourself before you purchase your horse is a wonderful way to establish a relationship.

So, how does a person go about meeting their new best friend? There are three things to keep in mind throughout the process: what you want, what you need, and what you can afford. Though it may seem like these objectives are flying far from each other in some cases, at some point, they will overlap to connect you with the right horse.

Let's take a look at what anyone shopping for their first or even fortieth horse needs to keep in mind when starting to dip their toes in the pools of horse ownership.

CHAPTER 1 : WHAT KIND OF HORSE DO YOU WANT?

Everyone has a dream horse, it seems. Even "non-horsey" people, who wouldn't take in a horse if they were giving them away free at the grocery store, tend to "ooh" and "ahh" a little over a horse now and again. Whether your tastes run more *Black Stallion* or *Misty of Chincoteague* says a lot about what kind of horse would be your dream companion.

Technically, every seasoned equestrian knows that deep down in the bottom of their heart, cosmetics don't matter as much as matching with a horse who you can safely work with and grow as a horse person. It's kind of like looking at a house and judging it based on the exterior paint color rather than whether it's well-constructed. A good horse should be a good companion first and foremost.

At the same time, there are scenarios in which cosmetic things are very important. For example, it's impossible to show at an American Quarter Horse Association (AQHA) sanctioned show on a horse that is not registered with AQHA. If you want to show Appaloosa or Palomino horses, you'll need a horse who demonstrates the breed qualities, including the distinctive coat colors. Additionally, if you will be showing your horse at high levels of competition, you'll want one that stands out from the rest of the pen in appearance or talent. Judges generally notice appearance first.

Therefore, it's not a bad idea to start with your dream horse when compiling a list of qualities you'd like to see in your new equine friend. As long as you realize you're more than likely going to have to compromise on a few of these features, having a dream is definitely not a bad thing.

Building Your Dream Horse

First, what breed of horse do you want? What breed of horse takes your breath away? Is it the feathery Friesian with its dashing black coat? Is it the sleek and athletic Thoroughbred, or the sturdy-yet-agile Quarter Horse? Maybe the unique breeds call to you such as the Bashkir Curly horse with its signature wavy coat or the Akal-Teke with its metallic sheen. Horse breeds are largely very distinct, and studying appearances, qualities, and abilities of various breeds will help you narrow your preferences.

Perhaps it's the color of the horse that strikes your fancy. I personally love a loud, splashy coat color. I once had the pleasure of showing a palomino Appaloosa named "Maximum Pixels." We definitely stood out in the show pen and had a blast. We met a lot of friends that day who wanted to pat Max to see if his coat "really looked like that." As the person who had stayed up the night before scrubbing grass stains out of the fine, blonde mane and tail, I assured them it was very real.

Some people believe the legends that red headed mares (chestnut or sorrel, depending on the breed registry) are zesty, opinionated divas and either gravitate towards or away from them based on this anecdotal analysis. Many people find grey horses striking, or love the way a horse with blue eyes looks. Whether you're Team Unicorn or searching for The Pie from *National Velvet,* you might just have a particular look you're interested in creating with your new horse.

The size of the beast also matters when dreaming of perfection. Some people are drawn to small, huggable ponies, especially if there are young riders or future equestrians in the picture. Others are attracted to large, bulky work horses, such as Percherons or Clydesdales. Whether you want something leggy or something that won't require a leg up to get on, we all have visions of strolling through a sunny pasture on what we consider the ideal steed.

The Dream Horse's Dream Job

Then again, you might want your horse to be able to do a particular job. If you're dabbling in dressage, you might gravitate towards a Prix St. George trained warmblood with big, expressive movement. Those who are getting serious about gymkhana might dream of a spitfire little compact pony who can run like the devil's after him.

Or your ideal horse might be the exact opposite of a highly-trained athlete. Maybe you're looking for a horse who will lumber along the trails with you, content as you are to wander without plans. A horse who has a sense of humor and doesn't mind when you lose your balance a little, or get really tense and accidentally pop him in the mouth.

Regardless of what your dream horse does for a living, you probably want him to be the very best at it. You want to continue to ride, compete, or just spend time with your new horse for a very long time. Those starting out in a particular sport might want a horse that's already trained to perform several levels above their current capabilities so that they can learn and progress on the same horse. Those who just want an equine companion might yearn for a younger horse, so they can grow old together. We create our dream horse based around the life we want to have together.

I won't tell you that a dream horse is "just a dream." Sometimes, people get exactly what they wish for, and it's a fairy tale come true. If you're looking for a bay horse, at least 50% Thoroughbred with Secretariat in his bloodlines and at least 16 hands high with hunter experience, I'm very confident that you will find several options available to you. But if you're looking for a grulla Paint/Belgian cow pony, you might have to wait for a while before you meet your dream horse or breed it yourself.

I won't tell anyone to give up on their dreams, because in the horse world, it seems like anything can happen. Instead, I'll ask you to really consider what you want. If you are in the enviable position to have multiple horses and the skills required to work with your dream horse, I say "go for it!" But if you're on a strict budget, you might need to consider compromising some of what you *want* for what you really *need* in a suitable equine companion.

CHAPTER 2 : WHAT KIND OF HORSE DO YOU NEED?

Serious question: What would you really do if someone dropped a fully unbroke Arabian stallion off at your house? Or a wild island pony with a baby by her side? It may sound heroic and heartwarming on the pages of our beloved childhood books, but if you are hoping to qualify for year-end Champion, divisional High Point, USDF Medals, or have any lofty goals besides keeping your horse alive, either of these equines appearing unannounced might be a cause for panic.

Sometimes, your dream horse is almost the exact embodiment of what you don't need at this moment in your life or equine career. I had the opportunity to purchase a 17 hand, Preliminary Level-trained Thoroughbred/draft eventer… at the exact moment I was putting my riding career on pause after a serious injury. Even though it was my dream horse, I wasn't sure if I was able to ride professionally. It would be unfair to both of us if I wasn't ready.

Therefore, it may turn out that the horse you want and the horse that makes sense for your current needs are a little more distant than you had hoped. I recommend taking some time to really consider what you need in a horse and figure out how you can compromise rather than dumping the entire plan. Those who have been around a variety of horses will share old adages like "you don't ride beauty; you ride the brain," or "a bloodline means nothing without training." There is a lot of truth in these statements, and I encourage you to keep them in mind when you're considering what you really want in a horse. At the end of the day, all of these things truly do matter. It's just a matter of determining what matters the most to you.

When it comes to choosing the right horse for your needs, I recommend taking a very strong look at the horse's size, temperament, skill, and training level above all other factors. All of these will help you find a horse that is practical for where you are in your life, so you can plan for your future equestrian career.

Let's take a closer look:

Size

The size of the horse can be very important, or barely important, depending on what you plan to do with it. If you're searching for a horse who will eat your grass, give you a good reason to be outside, and be a confidant to talk to who might just listen, any size horse will do. I simply recommend that you research how much food is appropriate for that horse, including pasture. Overfeeding a horse can be just as dangerous as underfeeding a horse.

If your horse will have a particular job, however, you'll want to consider the physical demands of that job. For example, if you're interested in jumping or eventing, you'll want a horse with the size and scope to jump larger fences and adjust their stride easily. A contesting horse will need to be nimble and responsive with fantastic balance. A-Circuit hunters have a very even, solid stride and a tidy jump. Concours d'Elegance carriage horses have an upright head position with expressive movement. Even if you plan to train your horse to perform the tasks you enjoy, there are certain restrictions to what physics will allow. For example, small horses have trouble getting over long courses of very big fences. Start your relationship with your new horse right by choosing a horse who is physically capable of doing what you demand of him on a regular basis.

Then, there is the matter of the size of the horse in relation to the size of the rider. There are many schools of thought on this matter, and a lot of feelings get hurt when the topic is mentioned. I believe that each horse needs to be considered as an individual when it comes to how much it can carry on its back or pull safely in harness. The famous "20% Rule" indicates that a horse should be comfortable carrying no more than 20% of its body weight on its back, including saddle and equipment.

However, a horse's conformation, lifestyle, athleticism, and training can have bearing on this. A solidly built horse with no lameness issues in the peak of training can do things a horse the same height– but out of shape and not in constant work– could not do. That's like saying that all people who are 5'6" should be able to deadlift 100 pounds. Size doesn't necessarily correlate to fitness.

Furthermore, this concept applies to riders as well. A heavier rider with an experienced seat will be less of a burden than an inexperienced thin rider who bounces all over a horse's back. A rider who is too tall for a smaller pony, but has a kind seat and great timing, might have a better ride than a shorter but less skilled rider. The horse will tell you if size is a problem by refusing to move, acting up by prancing or backing up quickly, or stumbling.

Size is very important when it comes to buying a horse for children, especially beginners. Children are difficult to shop for in general, since it's hard to predict when a growth spurt is going to happen. But when it comes to buying a horse, always keep in mind that the horse isn't going to change size.

Buying a horse that is too big for a child can be a challenge, since short, lightly muscled legs aren't necessarily as effective as the longer legs of an adult. I have worked with some very talented young riders, so I'm not indicating that children are poor riders, but that a very wide or tall horse can be difficult for those with shorter or smaller legs to sit on, squeeze, kick, and so forth. You always want to feel balanced and securely seated on a horse, regardless of the length of your legs or the number of years spent in the saddle.

But, selecting a pony that will eventually be outgrown offers its own set of problems. You need to be able to magically predict if your child will be the right size and skill level to enjoy this particular beast as well as come up with a plan for what the pony will do once he is too small for his intended rider. Ponies have this habit of living for thirty-plus years, and seem to grow more ornery with age, which makes future planning for such a creature a bit difficult.

If you find yourself in the same confusing spot as many parents, I strongly recommend enlisting the help of a professional to help you find the best equine companion for your child. They will be more connected with options in a specific discipline or community, and can help guide you through the tough "should I or shouldn't I?" decisions that come with figuring out which pony fits in your child's "Goldilocks" spot— that is, not too big and not too little.

Temperament

"Not too big and not too little" is a good way to describe your ideal horse's temperament as well. Some people prefer to ride a very hot, opinionated horse that can be unpredictable. Other people prefer a Steady Eddy who's seen it all twice and didn't care the first time he saw it. I refer to it as the horse's "Spice Level," because most people have a certain amount of equine zest they can physically handle, but they'd prefer even less than that. You don't want to be bored when you work with your horse, but you also don't want to be terrified. The primary reason we play with horses in the first place is because we enjoy it. There is no shame in choosing a horse because you know you will enjoy working with him.

If you're going to be showing or competing, you probably want a horse who has a competitive edge. My former racehorse Red is a great example of the exact opposite of a competitive edge: his trainers retired him from racing because he occasionally chose not to participate in the race at all. Your horse should want the blue as much as you do. He should approach obstacles boldly, make good decisions about where to put his feet, have the talent to do what is asked of him, and the focus to allow both his natural skills and training shine.

The opposite of this is also true. If you're mainly keeping your horse as a pet, make sure he's okay with that plan. Some horses get bored very easily, and the more bored a horse gets, the more creative they become. Horses express their boredom in many ways, but some of the most popular reactions include naughtiness: gates unlatched, fences chewed on, stall walls kicked down, and so forth. Keep your horse sane by making sure his temperament matches the lifestyle you have intended for him.

Skills and Training

Skills and training are two different traits in a horse. "Skill" refers to what a specific horse can do naturally, such as jump over things that are 5 feet tall or pace a mile in a specific amount of time. Therefore, "training," refers to what we do with a horse to help foster those skills.

I truly believe that horses can be trained to do just about anything, but for some of them, their skills are not specifically aligned with certain performance goals. Some of these reasons are biological; for example, the naturally upright head position and tight-kneed trot of the Hackney is not ideal for someone trying to show Western Pleasure, with its quiet, flat-legged gaits.

Just as humans have different areas where we both excel or find serious challenges, some horses are not suited for a particular job, despite everything adding up on paper. I'm really happy to write books about my nerdy interest in horses, but I could not write a sci-fi thriller, despite my enduring respect for the genre. Red's father was a multi-million dollar winning racehorse. Red quit after nine races.

Many times I see people who seem to think you can train a horse into what you want it to be. This is simply not universally true. You can train a horse to be the best it can be, based on its skills, temperament, and size, but just as not everyone is destined for an Olympic podium or Nobel Prize, not every horse is going to the top of its chosen sport.

But then again, neither is every rider.

When it comes to choosing the horse you need, I strongly suggest you be realistic with your riding goals. If you are looking at Grand Prix jumpers, but you've just started going over ground poles, I encourage you to re-examine your immediate needs. Likewise, if you're showing at a Grand Prix level, you should be looking at a horse that has at least been started over fences and that shows potential to hit the higher levels.

I'm not saying it's impossible, as there are many ponies who are quite successful at high level dressage, Standardbred barrel racers, and gaited eventing horses. Instead, I recommend that you choose a horse who is ready and willing to do the same things you want to do. Any horse can (and should!) be trained to do a variety of jobs, but as responsible and empathetic horse owners, we need to recognize that sometimes our goals do not align with the abilities of our equine companions.

Therefore, I encourage you to pause for a moment or two when you see your dream horse manifest before your eyes. Murphy's Law applies to the horse world as well, so it's very likely that the exact horse you were shopping for at a certain stage of your equine career will appear at the worst possible time.

When this happens, your inner horse-crazy kid will likely start screaming "PONY! PONY! PONY!" while making grabby hands. Reach inside yourself to consult with the responsible adult who pays all of the bills to truly consider whether this is a wise step for you and the horse. If you are in an enviable position where you have the capacity and budget for several horses at the same time, go for it. If your list of wants and needs overlap in enough places that you can safely and happily work with your slightly imperfect dream horse, go for it.

But if you find yourself calling in favors, pulling strings, and rearranging a lot of moving pieces to make it work, I encourage you to consider this a sign from The Universe (or any external force of your choosing) that it was not meant to be. There are hundreds upon thousands of horses in this world. If you are active in the horse community, either through showings, trails, breed associations, or riding clubs and meet-ups, you will encounter a lot of horses. You will fall in love with almost all of them. Before you go all starry-eyed and senseless over a horse who meets your absolute ideal, I recommend using a basic rating system to determine if you should allow your emotions to drive.

For example, I adhere to this system:

Sensibility Level 1: Horse is completely unsuitable for me. Bringing this horse into my life would be dangerous, bankrupting, or require a complete overhaul of my lifestyle. Admire the horse. Pat the horse. Walk away.

Sensibility Level 2: Probably not the best idea, but could be a fun project for a few months. Horse will need a new owner in a few months to a year. Do not expect an ROI (return on investment). Do not get super attached.

Sensibility Level 3: Horse would make a good part-time or short-term horse. He could be fun for a certain purpose, and I could lease him out so he gets more work and attention. Wait, why am I buying a horse if I'm just going to lease it out? Maybe I should think about this.

Sensibility Level 4: Unnecessary but purposeful purchase. He's a reasonably wise investment for my current skill level and equine interaction needs. Not a huge drain on bank account or lifestyle, either. I could ride the fence on this decision for a few more months, but at some point I'll have to make up my mind.

Sensibility Level 5: Good fit overall. May not check all of the boxes in the "Needs" section, but the gaps between what I need and what this horse offers are great opportunities for each of us to learn. There's nothing I can't work through with a good trainer. Looking forward to spending significant time together, and hey– maybe we'll end up making a really great team!

Sensibility Level 6: The Universe and all of the deities have aligned to put this horse in my life at this exact moment. There might be a few slight imperfections, but they only enhance the magnetic soul connection I have with this horse. Get on the trailer, Fluffy; we're going home.

It's not always as simple as this. Red, for example, was a Level 1 when I met him. He was neglected, lame, underweight, and therefore impossible to evaluate sufficiently under saddle. For some reason, however, he lit up my Level 6 button. However, I was at a point in my life where I could invest time and money into seeing this through.

Which brings us to the next important consideration of your horse purchasing process: How much are you willing to invest in this horse?

CHAPTER 3 : WHAT KIND OF HORSE CAN YOU AFFORD?

I say "afford," but money is only part of the investment you'll make in your new horse. Horses require time. They need regular attention. They will make you laugh, cry, scream, and feel a whirlwind of emotions you didn't even know could go together. That's part of why we like these strange beasts after all.

Therefore, when you think about words like "afford," "cost," or any other terms that are typically reserved for financial transactions, I ask that you think about the time and emotional investments as well.

People ask me all the time, "how much does a horse cost?" And my response is always "as much as you're willing to give." You can always spend more money on your horse. That's why they make saddle pads and polo wraps in many styles and colors. But seriously, the value and the price of a horse aren't always in sync, and like many markets, the dollar means different things based on the season, training, current competition, and so on. And when you factor in the emotional requirements? I can't think of a better way to put it than, "as much as you're willing to give."

So, how do you budget for a horse with these things in mind?

Start researching. Check out online horse magazines or want ads, horse sales pages like Dreamhorse.com or equinenow.com, and even your breed and local horse community forums are a good place to see current horse prices. Many of the online sales pages have filters that allow you to select the dimensions and price range for your dream horse as well as notes on temperament, skills, and training. You would think that this would make it easy, but it does not. One factor will always be out of alignment with the rest, and unless you have limitless funds at your disposal, it will be the price.

Horses can cost hundreds of thousands of dollars. People also give away horses for free. The likelihood of these horses being of the same caliber of temperament, training, and skills is small. Though there are slimy trainers and less-than-truthful horse flippers out there, "you get what you pay for" is a generally reasonable guideline. A horse with more than four digits in its price tag is generally going to have impeccable breeding, ribbon-winning talent, and training to encourage and enhance this talent. According to cowboy philosophy, a free horse is nothing but a $100,000 vet bill. Make your decision wisely.

Speaking of outrageous vet bills, I cannot encourage a vet check strongly enough. When you purchase a horse, call a trusted equine vet to complete a pre-purchase exam (PPE). This will cost you money, but can help you walk away from a situation that might be very bad for you and the horse in the long run. Before you buy the horse, a vet will come out to gauge its overall health, soundness, take X-rays, and even run blood samples for evidence of drugging or disease in some cases.

Why do you want the vet to come out to do all of this when you can see for yourself that the horse looks great and happy? Because it might not be great and happy once you get it home. There is no return policy with most horses. Once you trailer it off the property, it's generally expected that it will stay there, unless your sales contract has a buy-back clause or First Right of Refusal notation. In those cases, yes, you can contact the previous owner to decide what to do.

Therefore, when you start riding Fluffy regularly, and his old coffin bone injury that was never disclosed starts acting up, you have a problem. When you walk into the barn to feed your new mare and discover two heads in the stall instead of one, congratulations on your new foal– which is now your problem. When the mild-mannered horse becomes a raging Hell-beast once the Acepromazine wears off or the HYPP tremors begin, you'll wish you had known about these issues before you bought the horse. A PPE will help reveal all of these things, so that you know ahead of time whether or not you should purchase this horse.

Health problems can be manageable, but they can impact your relationship and career with your horse as well as throw off your budget. Not all future injuries or illnesses can be revealed through a PPE. In fact, if someone invents a test that predicts colic, I will give you all of my money— but knowing about previous injuries and existing problems at the time of purchase can help you make informed decisions. That way you won't have an expensive emotional crisis on your hands when the horse you love suddenly isn't suitable anymore.

Also bear in mind that horses are ongoing expenses. They eat every day. In fact, they eat a lot every day. They need a place to live. They need daily attention and maintenance. You need to exercise them. If your horse will be boarded at a nearby facility, you will need to pay for transportation to said facility which can include gasoline, mileage on your car, and long hours spent horsing around.

Can you do this for a long time? You may be very willing now, but that can change. Life has a funny way of throwing weird things in our paths at completely unexpected times. What will you do with your horse if your job relocates you, or you get pregnant, or your schedule changes?

It's okay to not be able to afford a horse. It's okay to say "this is not the time for me to buy a horse." It's also okay to set guidelines so strict that any horse that makes it to Level 6 on the suitability scale is actual perfection. Obey your limits, whether that's money, time, or even your emotional state. If owning a horse is going to be a huge drain or a chore, perhaps this is not the right time for you.

I assure you, as a persistent and long-suffering horseless horse-crazy kid, that at some point, it will be the right time. I was 30 years old when I met Red, though I had been working with horses since age 7. In that time, I had met, worked with, and built relationships with plenty of horses. I leased a few, and I did some catch riding in college, in which I rode whatever beast was handed to me to the specifications of the owner. I learned so much that when Red came trotting into my life, it really was like Heaven and Earth had aligned to bring us together. Not to get too sappy, but sometimes it isn't meant to be, and sometimes everything plays out exactly as it should.

Author's Anecdote: What If It Doesn't Work Out?

Many years ago, I worked at a farm that rescued and rehabilitated horses. Seeing the horses come into our care in various states of neglect and starvation was hard enough, but often, it was compounded by the tragic tales told by the owners surrendering their horses. "Well, my daughter outgrew her, and I didn't know what to do with her, so I just left her out in the field for a year." Or, "We got him for our son, but he wanted to do speed events, and this horse just isn't fast. We got our son another horse and just kept him around for company, but now he's mean."

In most cases, people buy an unsuitable horse out of the best of intentions. It was perfect when they got it, but then things changed. They switched disciplines, stopped riding, grew up, or became overwhelmed with work/school/life. These are very real circumstances, and I would like to encourage anyone who finds themselves unable to care for their horses the way they need to receive care to do the right thing and sell or rehome your horse.

That being said, we were known for getting some of the "worst of the worst" cases in our county: An entire herd of inbred horses who had never been handled. A former barrel racing champ who had stood in a field for a year, losing her mind with boredom. Many green-broke horses who were once 4H projects but were immediately dumped once the kid lost interest in it. These horses had been without proper handling and nutrition for so long, they often needed months of care before they were healthy enough to evaluate for training.

I encourage you to think long and hard about your dream horse. Your new equine companion has no choice in the decision. Once you pay the fee, the horse is legally yours to do what you want with him. However, both of your lives will proceed more smoothly if you make that horse a promise to do what is right for both of you.

If it doesn't work out for any reason, make the tough decisions. If you can't afford more than one horse, find your first buddy a new home. That might take the form of leasing him, selling him, or finding a local rescue organization that can help you rehome him. There is no shame in any of these options, though you might be very sad and even guilty that you are making the best choice for both of you to continue on your path. Shake hands, hug, give him a treat, and allow both you and your horse to move forward with your lives.

CONCLUSION

You will find your dream horse. He might end up looking a lot different than your imaginary Black Beauty or Pegasus. You might find yourself walking out your horse at the end of a great work session thinking, "How did I end up with this critter?" You might walk into the barn and wonder, "Is this horse really mine?" when your beast pokes his head out of his stall, eager to spend time with you. And sometimes, you might be tempted to list your horse for sale when he's being especially naughty or difficult.

That's how you know you've got the right horse. When you feel as many mixed emotions about your equine partner as you do about your human family, it's a good sign that you have chosen wisely. Of course, some families are more complicated than others, but when you look back on your relationship with your horse, many years from now, are you going to smile with warm recollection? If so, then this is the right horse.

Going into the horse shopping process with specific goals will help increase the chances of having a positive relationship with your horse. While it's impossible to predict the future, paying close attention to what you want, what you need, and what you can afford will guide you towards making better decisions when purchasing a horse.

A horse is— both literally and figuratively— a big investment. I strongly recommend working with your trainer or another trusted equine professional if this is your first time purchasing a horse, or if you're new to a certain discipline or sport. It's important to be able to read between the lines of sales ads, to have a keen eye for detail in observing a horse's movement and behavior, and to have an expert's opinion on how much you might pay for this horse.

While we like to think sellers are honest, sometimes they're sadly misinformed. For example, I had a seller try to sell me a Thoroughbred gelding for a very high price based on his bloodlines. A gelding is a castrated male horse. They cannot breed. His bloodlines were completely irrelevant. He was also completely untrained and 300 pounds underweight, things the current owner was not aware of because she had very little information or interaction with horses in general. Had I not had expertise on the matter, I would've ended up paying a lot of money for a lot of problems. Instead, I paid a reasonable amount of money for a lot of problems I was capable of handling and remedying.

The bottom line to knowing how to select the perfect horse for your life is to know your own capabilities and limits. While getting what you want is very important to the overall equation, finding a horse that meets your needs and that you can easily afford is much more important to the long-term relationship the two of you are about to build.

So, now what? If this is your first horse, or you're new to the horse world, I strongly encourage you to check out *Before Your Horse Comes Home: Introductory Horse Care for Beginners* and *I Have a Horse… Now What : How Grooming, Training, Riding, and Equine Competitive Activities Can Build a Lifelong Bond*.

Before Your Horse Comes Home: Introductory Horse Care for Beginners details what it takes to keep a horse healthy and happy. Whether you're keeping your horse at home, looking for a boarding barn, or are unsure which option best suits your needs, *Before Your Horse Comes Home: Introductory Horse Care for Beginners* contains information regarding what a horse needs to thrive.

In *I Have a Horse… Now What : How Grooming, Training, Riding, and Equine Competitive Activities Can Build a Lifelong Bond*, we dive deeper into the relationship you're about to forge with your new equine companion. From groundwork and learning how to like each other to finding new sports and activities to enjoy as a team, *I Have a Horse… Now What : How Grooming, Training, Riding, and Equine Competitive Activities Can Build a Lifelong Bond* encourages interaction with your horse in a way that makes sense for both you and your buddy.

I am confident that the stars will align, and you will find your dream horse in your lifetime. And when you do, I wish the two of you many great years together as you learn, grow, and enjoy each other's presence.

Happy trails!

DOWNLOAD YOUR FREE CHECKLIST NOW!

Horse owners are often accused of having too much stuff, and yet we always find ourselves without that One Thing that we really, really need. This list is intended to keep the new horse owner organized so you have a head start on your own collection of "stuff."

Go to **https://free.meredithhillbook.com/checklist** to download it for free

REVIEWS

Reviews and feedback help improve this book and the author. If you enjoy this book, we would greatly appreciate it if you could take a few moments to share your opinion and post a review on Amazon.

Download The Audio Version of This Book for Free! If you love listening to audiobooks on-the-go or enjoy the narration as you read along I have great news for you. You can download this book for **FREE** just by signing up for a FREE 30-day audible trial. Just use the links below

FOR AUDIBLE UK:

https://tinyurl.com/4ze6thhu

FOR AUDIBLE US:

https://tinyurl.com/2ma8erme

ALSO BY MEREDITH HILL

Before Your Horse Comes Home

http://mybook.to/horses

www.ingramcontent.com/pod-product-compliance
Lightning Source LLC
Chambersburg PA
CBHW071424070526
44578CB00003B/683